LET LOOSE ON MOTHER GOOSE

by Terry Graham

ACTIVITIES TO TEACH MATH, SCIENCE, ART, MUSIC, LIFE SKILLS & LANGUAGE DEVELOPMENT

INCENTIVE PUBLICATIONS, INC.

Library of Congress Catalog Number: # 81-80248
ISBN # 0-86530-030-5

INTRODUCTION

My love of "Mother Goose" comes from my mother and grand-mother, who loved the rhymes themselves and read them to me over and over. Because of them, I knew nearly all the nursery rhymes before I ever went to school. I didn't know what words like "tuffet" or "curds and whey" meant, or what it was that Jack broke when he fell. I only knew that the verses delighted me with their rhythms and rhymes; and because I loved them, they became a part of me. As I grew up, I realized that the rhymes were part of my heritage — a portion of the poetic tradition shared by almost all English-speaking people.

This awareness prompted me to draw on the common bond of nursery rhyme knowledge when I entered the teaching profession. The activities in this book were developed around "Mother Goose" as part of a curriculum to teach math, science, art, music, life skills and language development. With "Mother Goose," my success was assured for two reasons. First, many students already knew the rhymes, so their familiarity gave them confidence to expand their knowledge. Secondly, students who did not know the verses were enchanted, as I was, by the sound, the imagery, the language and the humor of the rhymes, and this made them eager to learn.

Every child should have the chance to experience and grow from the wonderful world of "Mother Goose." And so I dedicate this book, with many thanks, to all the children I have taught and the many more who have taught me, and to "Mother Goose," who reminds us:

> Monday's child is fair of face;
> Tuesday's child is full of grace.
> Wednesday's child is full of woe;
> Thursday's child has far to go.
> Friday's child is loving and giving;
> Saturday's child works hard for a living;
> And the child that is born on the Sabbath day
> Is bonnie and blythe and good and gay.

Terry Graham

NOTE: Material for the historical notes accompanying the nursery rhymes was condensed from various sources. For additional information, consult the books listed in the bibliography.

HOW TO USE
THIS BOOK

Create a "Mother Goose Pocket Rhyme Record" on a large piece of tag or poster board. Staple or glue on pockets made from construction paper, label them with rhyme names and finish with your own illustrations or with copies of the activity sheets from this book.

Display the rhyme record prominently in your classroom. Add children's art work, nursery rhyme books, posters, pictures and charts depicting nursery rhyme characters to the area.

When a child recites a rhyme, write his/her name or symbol on a wooden craft stick and help the child put it in the appropriate pocket.

Some children will not be able to recite because of speech, language and/or memory recall difficulties, or because of fear or shyness. Encourage shy children to recite in pairs or groups; ask other children to draw pictures and/or answer questions about the rhymes in their own ways. Accept whatever a child is able to give, and reward and praise every effort.

Do not put pressure on the children to recite. Reciting does allow many children to experience pride and gives them a feeling of accomplishment, but the important thing is to instill in every child the joy of reading and listening to nursery rhymes.

TABLE OF CONTENTS

HUMPTY DUMPTY

Humpty Dumpty sat on a wall;
Humpty Dumpty had a great fall.
All the king's horses and all the king's men
Couldn't put Humpty Dumpty together again!

HISTORY: The rhyme originated as a riddle. Humpty Dumpty is an egg, which is why he cannot be put together again.

Activities

INTRODUCTION

Ask each child to bring an egg to class. If eggs are carried to school in a cup or in part of an egg carton, even the smallest children can transport them safely.

Discuss color, size and shape of eggs. What is on the outside? inside? How do they smell? Are they hard or soft? What can we do with eggs?

MATH

Count the eggs. Put them into egg cartons. How many are in a dozen?

COOKING

A. *Humpty Dumpty Scrambled Eggs*

Help each child break an egg into a bowl. Children will enjoy using egg beaters, whisks or mixers to beat eggs. Add 2 tablespoons of milk. Pour mixture into well-greased skillet or electric fry pan. Children take turns stirring eggs. (Provide toast and juice and enjoy a nutritious brunch.)

B. *Humpty Dumpty's Pear Salad*

For each child, provide half a pear, a Lifesaver (or some kind of roll candy), 1 tablespoon mayonnaise, 2 cherries, a raisin and a lettuce leaf. Each child puts a lettuce leaf on a plate and places a pear half on top of it, round side up. Then, each child adds two cherries for eyes, a raisin for a nose and roll candy for a mouth. Add mayonnaise to taste.

ART

A. Give each child a piece of construction paper with wall drawn at bottom. Children can paste pre-cut shapes or trace their own from patterns.

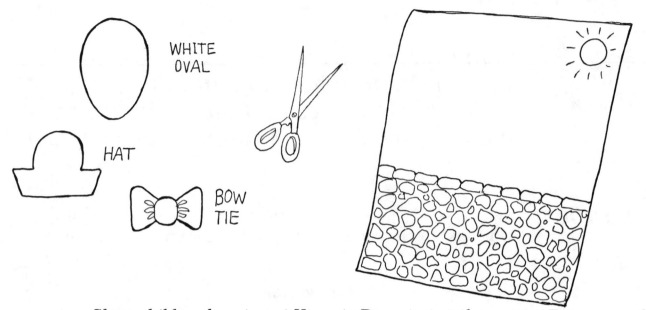

Show children how to put Humpty Dumpty together again. Encourage them to add facial features, arms and legs.

B. *Hard Boiled Humpty Dumpty*

Boil eggs in class and allow to cool. Children use magic markers to give Humpty Dumpty a face. Use scraps of material and yarn for hats, clothing and ties.

ORAL LANGUAGE DEVELOPMENT

Where did Humpty Dumpty sit? What happened to him? Who came to help him? Why couldn't he be put back together again?

CONCEPTS

Together/Apart

DRAMA

Ask for volunteers for the roles of Humpty Dumpty, the horses and the king's men. Children will enjoy acting out the rhyme as the audience recites it.

MUSIC

Sing the rhyme to the tune of "Twinkle, Twinkle, Little Star."

GAME

Divide the class into two relay teams. Give the first child on each team a hard boiled egg in a spoon. Holding one hand behind their backs, the two children race to a designated place and then return to their teams to give the egg in the spoon to the next child. The game continues in this manner until one team finishes to win the game. (If an egg is dropped, the team calls out, "Humpty Dumpty!" and that team is out.)

ACTIVITY SHEET

Reproduce and use.

HUMPTY DUMPTY

PETER, PETER, PUMPKIN EATER

Peter, Peter, pumpkin eater,
Had a wife and couldn't keep her.
He put her in a pumpkin shell
And there he kept her very well.

HISTORY: The pumpkin is a well-loved vegetable in children's literature. It was thought to have charms against evil spirits.

Activities

ART

Give each child a pumpkin pattern. Have him/her trace and cut out two pumpkins.

Have children staple the two pumpkins together at the stem. Cut pictures of "Peter's wife" from magazines. Let each child choose a picture to paste inside his/her pumpkin "shell." Children use crayons or markers to draw doors and windows on the outside of the pumpkin.

Glue words inside so that parents can reinforce the rhyme at home.

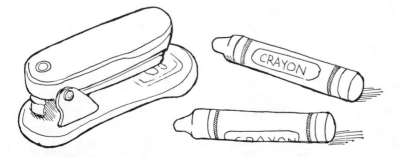

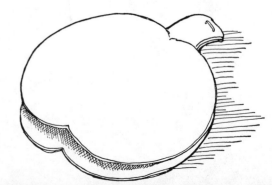

SCIENCE

Have a pumpkin-tasting party. Let children taste slices of the raw pumpkin; then fry some in butter, salt and pepper for a different taste.

ORAL LANGUAGE DEVELOPMENT

Who had a wife? Who was in the pumpkin shell? How was she kept? What words begin with the same sound as *Peter*? (Pumpkin, put)

GAMES

A. *Jack-O-Lantern Toss*

Use a jack-o-lantern with an over-sized mouth and pumpkin seeds for this game. Give each child some seeds to toss into the jack-o-lantern's mouth. (Variation: Have children toss walnuts or peanuts into the top of the pumpkin.)

B. *Steal the Pumpkin*

Place 2 medium-sized pumpkins at the center of the play area, with one team at one goal and the other team at another. One child from each team runs out and tries to roll the pumpkin back to the home goal before the other child does the same. Continue in this manner until every child on one team has rolled the pumpkin back to win the game.

ACTIVITY SHEET

Reproduce and use.

PETER, PETER, PUMPKIN EATER

LITTLE MISS MUFFET

Little Miss Muffet
Sat on a tuffet
Eating her curds and whey.
Along came a spider
Who sat down beside her
And frightened Miss Muffet away!

HISTORY: Some experts believe that Miss Muffet was Mary, Queen of Scots, and the spider was her enemy John Knox. But children love the rhyme for its lilting rhythm and because they identify with the frightened child.

Activities

ART
Give each child a 4" black circle and 8 strips of black paper. Show children how to glue the spider's "legs" onto the "body" circle, 4 on each side. Add a thin piece of elastic to the spider so that it can be dangled in front of Miss Muffet.

COOKING
Hey! Hey! Hey!
What ARE curds and whey?
Let's find out today!
   To make curds and whey, stir 2 cups whole milk over medium heat until it starts to bubble. Remove from heat, add 1 tablespoon of vinegar and continue stirring until curds form. Strain off the whey, squeezing out any remains with a spoon. Add a little salt and serve on crackers.

ORAL LANGUAGE DEVELOPMENT
Who sat on a tuffet? Who frightened Miss Muffet? Who ate curds and whey? Where did the spider go? What frightens YOU?

DRAWING CONCLUSIONS
Where did Miss Muffet go? What would the spider have said — if it could talk?

CONCEPTS

Beside   Away   On

DRAMA

Ask for volunteers to play the roles of Miss Muffet, the tuffet and the spider. (Give Miss Muffet a spoon and a bowl — and maybe even a hat.) Direct the rest of the class to recite the rhyme as the players dramatize it.

SCIENCE

Discuss insects and spiders. Explain that spiders are different from insects because spiders have four pairs of legs and insects only have three pairs of legs. Spiders belong to the family called "Arachnids."

Also help children find out why spiders make webs and how the silken threads of the web help to transport the spider.

MUSIC

Sing "Little Miss Muffet" to the tune of "Yankee Doodle."

GAME

Draw a circle about 3' in diameter on the ground or floor. Place a chair or low stool in the center of the circle. Select one child to represent "Miss Muffett," and seat the child on the chair. The other children are spiders who must hop into and out of "Miss Muffet's" circle without being tagged. "Miss Muffet" must remain on the "tuffet" at all times. If "Miss Muffet" tags another child, that child becomes "Miss Muffett" and the game continues.

ACTIVITY SHEET

Reproduce and use.

LITTLE MISS MUFFET

LITTLE JACK HORNER

Little Jack Horner
Sat in a corner
Eating a Christmas pie.
He stuck in his thumb
And pulled out a plum,
And said, "What a good boy am I!"

HISTORY: Jack Horner was said to have been Thomas Horner, who stole one of several deeds to manorial estates from inside a pie sent to Henry VIII from the Abbot Glastonbury. Children love the rhyme because it presents such an attractive scene — a child eating a whole pie without benefit of fork or spoon!

Activities

ART
Use this recipe to make "dough" for the children: 3 parts flour; 1 part salt; 2 tablespoons oil. Mix with water to desired consistency. Add blue and red food coloring to make purple dough for plums.

Give each child enough dough to make one large ball for a pie and one small ball for a plum. Children push their thumbs into center of large ball and pinch edges to create the "Christmas pie," and then place their "plums" in the center. Then say the rhyme together as each child portrays "Jack."

COOKING
Follow this recipe to make *Jack Horner's Christmas Pie*.

2-crust 9" pie shell	4 cups sliced purple plums
1/2 cup sugar	1 tablespoon lemon juice
1/3 cup all-purpose flour	2 tablespoons butter
1/2 teaspoon cinnamon	

Preheat oven to 425°. Stir flour, sugar and cinnamon together; mix with plums. Turn into pastry shell; sprinkle with lemon juice and dot with butter. Cover with top crust which has slits cut in it; seal and flute. Cover edge with a 2/3" strip of aluminum foil to prevent excessive browning; remove foil last 15 minutes of baking. Bake 35-45 minutes or until crust is brown and juice begins to bubble through slits in crust.

ORAL LANGUAGE DEVELOPMENT

Where did Jack sit? Which finger did he put in the pie? What did he pull out? What did he say? What rhymes with *Horner*? (corner) What rhymes with pie? (I)

CONCEPTS

In/Out

MUSIC

Use a piano or guitar to play the following tune. Teach it to the children and let them sing it together with you.

D D D G F
Little Jack Horner

E E E A G
Sat in a corner

F F F B A G G
Eating a Christmas pie

D D D D G
He stuck in his thumb

F E E E A
And pulled out a plum

High High High
G F E D C E F G G
And said, "What a good boy am I!"

GAME

Christmas Pie-Eating Contest

The children make pudding and put it in small paper muffin cups for Jack Horner's Christmas pie. Give each child one cup of pudding. Children must put their hands behind their backs and try to eat their "pies."

ACTIVITY SHEET

Reproduce and use.

LITTLE JACK HORNER

HEY DIDDLE, DIDDLE

Hey, Diddle, Diddle
The cat and the fiddle,
The cow jumped over the moon;
The little dog laughed
To see such sport,
And the dish ran away with the spoon.

HISTORY: The names in this rhyme might refer to members of the court of Elizabeth I. Elizabeth was sometimes called "The Cat." The "little dog" might have been her friend, Robert Dudley. The "dish" and "spoon" could have been the Earl of Hertford and Lady Catherine Grey, who eloped during her reign. However, other authorities consider it strictly a nonsense verse which enchants children with its rhythm and the ridiculous antics it presents.

Activities

INTRODUCTION

Use 4 sheets of tag or cardboard to make sequence illustrations to help children learn this rhyme. Punch 2 holes at the top of each page. Use yarn or metal rings to hold the pages together, and flip them as the children recite the rhyme.

ART

Fold 2 pieces of 9" x 12" construction paper in half and staple one side to create a book for each child. Write the words "Hey Diddle, Diddle" on each cover (or help children do this).

Encourage children to illustrate the covers and to print their names on them.

On page 1, each child draws a cat and a fiddle and adds a rubber band to the fiddle so it can be plucked. On page 2, each child draws a cow and a moon (or cuts cow and moon from construction paper) and glues into place. On page 3, each child draws a little dog (or cuts one from greeting cards or magazines) and glues into place. On page 4, each child glues a small paper plate and plastic spoon. Encourage children to draw faces on and add arms and legs to the dish and the spoon.

ORAL LANGUAGE DEVELOPMENT

Who played the fiddle? What did the cow do? Who ran away with the spoon? What happened first? second? third? fourth?

CONCEPTS

Sequence   Over   Away

DRAMA

Ask for volunteers to play the roles of the cat, the cow, the dish, the dog, the moon and the spoon. Before the exercise, discuss with the children the way the cat plays the fiddle, how the dog laughs and a way to make your body into the shape of the moon. After this discussion, let the volunteers act out the rhyme while the rest of the children narrate it in unison. (Be sure to have enough space so that the dish and the spoon can run away.)

MUSIC

Sing "Hey Diddle, Diddle" to the tune of "Skip to My Lou" following this format.

Hey diddle, diddle, the cat and the fiddle ...
Hey diddle, diddle, the cat and the fiddle ...
Hey diddle, diddle, the cat and the fiddle ...
　　The cow jumped over the moon.

The little dog laughed to see such sport ...
The little dog laughed to see such sport ...
The little dog laughed to see such sport ...
　　And the dish ran away with the spoon.

ACTIVITY SHEET

Reproduce and use.

HEY DIDDLE, DIDDLE

JACK AND JILL

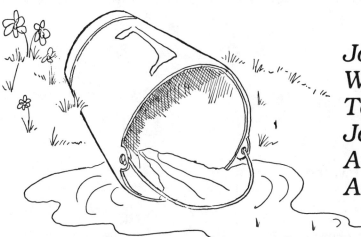

Jack and Jill
Went up the hill
To fetch a pail of water.
Jack fell down
And broke his crown
And Jill came tumbling after.

HISTORY: Early illustrations of this rhyme show two boys, possibly Cardinal Wolsey and Bishop Tarbes, supposedly on their way ("up the hill") to arrange the marriage of Mary Tudor to the French monarch. The pail of water might mean the holy water of the Popeship, an office that Wolsey wanted.

Activities

ART
Give each child a piece of construction paper with a hill drawn on it.

Show children how to tear pieces of green tissue paper, crush them into balls and glue onto the hill. Ask children to draw Jack and Jill going up or coming down the hill.

ORAL LANGUAGE DEVELOPMENT
Who went up the hill? Who fell down? Who came tumbling after? Why did they go up the hill?

CONCEPTS
Up/Down   After

29

MUSIC

Use a guitar or a piano to play the following tune. Teach it to the children and let them sing it with you.

```
        High              High
    C   G   A   G     C   G   G
   Jack and Jill went  up  the hill
```

```
        High High High
    G     E     D     C     B     A   G
   To   fetch   a    pail   of  water.
```

```
          High                    High
    F    F    D    F    E    E     C
   Jack fell down and broke his crown
```

```
                 Low
    E    D    A    G    D    D C
   And Jill came tumbling after.
```

MOVEMENT

A. After the children have learned the song, teach them the following movements to accompany it.

Jack and Jill went up the hill	(March — lift knees high)
To fetch a pail of water	(Bend over; rest top of head on floor)
Jack fell down and broke his crown	(Somersault)
And Jill came tumbling after	(Continue somersaults)

B. Provide a soft rug or tumbling mat. Help children do somersaults and simple tumbling stunts.

GAMES

A. *Jacks vs. Jills*

Divide the class into "Jacks" and "Jills" for this relay. Give the first child in each group a small plastic cup filled with water. Each child holds the cup with both hands and jumps to the finish line. Each child then runs back to his/her team and gives the cup to the next child. The team with more water left in the cup after each child has had a turn wins the relay.

B. *Potato Pail*

Divide the class into 3 teams. Provide 12 potatoes (4 for each team). The first child on each team is blindfolded and tries to throw the 4 potatoes into the pail. The child then takes a second turn without the blindfold. The game continues until all team members have had a chance to participate. One point is scored for each potato that lands in the pail, and the team with the highest score wins the game.

ACTIVITY SHEET

Reproduce and use.

JACK AND JILL

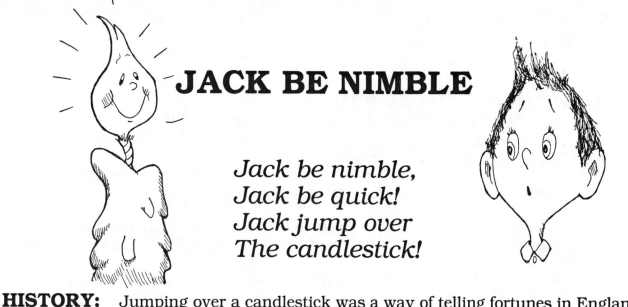

JACK BE NIMBLE

Jack be nimble,
Jack be quick!
Jack jump over
The candlestick!

HISTORY: Jumping over a candlestick was a way of telling fortunes in England. When a person jumped over a lighted candle without putting out the flame, he or she was assured of good luck for a full year.

Activities

ART

Give each child a piece of construction paper, and direct children to draw a spiral at the bottom of the paper.

Give children pre-cut yellow paper strips and red or orange flames to glue onto the spiral candlestick holder.

Type the rhyme (or write it in big letters) and reproduce one copy for each child. Let the children glue the rhyme to the top of the page.

Ask children to draw Jack as he jumps over the candlestick.

33

ORAL LANGUAGE DEVELOPMENT

A. Bring a candle to class, and discuss the following questions.

  What is a candle made from?
  Why did people of long ago need candles?
  What other things do we know of that are made from wax or have wax in
    them? (crayons, paper cups and plates, floor wax, etc.)

B. What other word in the rhyme begins with the same sound as "Jack"?
  Can you think of other words that rhyme with "nimble"? (thimble, cymbal,
  tremble, etc.)
  What other words rhyme with "quick"? (sick, tick, lick, kick, pick, etc.)

MUSIC
Teach "Jack Be Nimble" to the tune of "Are You Sleeping?"

DRAMA
Bring a candle and candlestick to class. Allow the children to take turns jumping
over it. As each child jumps, direct the class to recite the rhyme, substituting the
jumping child's name in the place of "Jack."

MOVEMENT
Light the candle, and direct the children to watch what happens to the wax and
the flame. Then, ask the children to pretend they are lighted candles and move to
show the flickering of the flame and the melting of the wax. (Music to "melt" to:
"Beethoven's Piano Concerto #5, 2nd Movement — Adagio un Poco Mosso.")

LIFE SKILLS
Remind the children that fire is a very dangerous thing. Impress upon them that
they should never try this experiment or play with fire in any form unless they are
supervised by an adult.

SCIENCE
Invite a resource person to demonstrate candle-making for the children, or take a
field trip to a craft center so children can view candles being made.

GAME
The children stand in a circle formation. One child volunteers to be "Jack," and
stands in the center of the circle. All of the children say the rhyme. At the last
word, "Jack" jumps between two children in the circle. Those children run in
opposite directions around the circle. The first child who returns to his/her place
becomes the new "Jack," and the game continues.

ACTIVITY SHEET
Reproduce and use.

JACK BE NIMBLE

BAA, BAA, BLACK SHEEP

Baa, baa, black sheep,
  Have you any wool?
Yes, sir, yes, sir,
  Three bags full.
One for my master,
  And one for my dame,
And one for the little boy
  Who lives down the lane.

HISTORY: This rhyme is thought to be a complaint made by commoners because of the excessive amount of wool that went to the king and the nobility.

Activities

ART

A. Give each child a pattern or pre-cut sheep. Have children glue pieces of cotton to the sheep and then sprinkle powdered black tempera paint over the cotton.

B. Have the children cover paper with black fingerpaint. When the paint is dry, cut into sheep shapes.

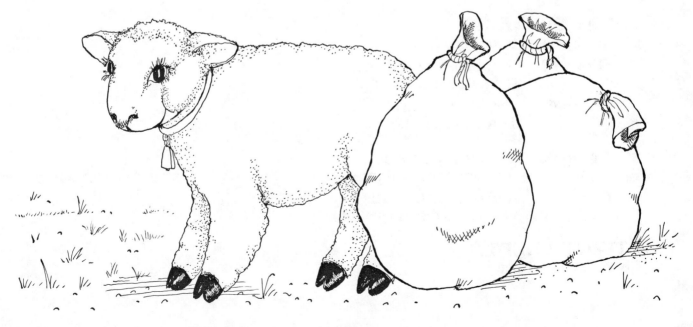

SCIENCE

Bring samples of wool to class. Encourage the children to describe its texture and tell some of its uses.

DRAMA

Provide grocery bags and crumpled newspaper (for wool). Divide the children into 3 groups. See which group can fill the bags first. Then, from the winning team, ask for volunteers to play the roles of the black sheep and the narrator.

ORAL LANGUAGE DEVELOPMENT

What sound does a sheep make? How many bags of wool did the sheep have? Who were the bags of wool for? Where did the little boy live?

MUSIC

Sing "Baa, Baa, Black Sheep" to the tune of "Twinkle, Twinkle, Little Star."

GAME

Wool Toss

Give each child a cotton ball. Designate a mark behind which the children must stand. See who can throw the cotton ball the farthest. (Variation: Provide a can or bucket for children to toss the cotton ball into.)

MOVEMENT

Direct the children to stand in a circle. Teach them the following movements.

Baa, Baa, Black Sheep	(Stamp 3 times)
Have you any wool?	(Shake forefinger 3 times)
Yes, sir, yes, sir,	(Nod head twice)
Three bags full.	(Hold up 3 fingers)
One for my master,	(Bow to the person on the right)
And one for my dame,	(Bow to the person on the left)
And one for the little boy	(Hold up 1 finger)
Who lives down the lane.	(Each child turns in a circle and ends facing center)

CHORAL SPEAKING

Divide the class into 2 groups.

Group #1: Baa, baa, black sheep,
           Have you any wool?

Group #2: Yes, sir, yes, sir,
           Three bags full.

Group #2: One for my master,
           And one for my dame,

Group #1: And one for the little boy
           Who lives down the lane.

ACTIVITY SHEET

Reproduce and use.

BAA, BAA, BLACK SHEEP

MISTRESS MARY

Mary

Mistress Mary, quite contrary,
How does your garden grow?
With silver bells and cockle shells
And pretty maids all in a row.

HISTORY: "Mary" is supposed to be Mary, Queen of Scots, and the "pretty maids" are her ladies-in-waiting. "Cockle shells" may have been dress decorations.

Activities

ART

A. Obtain wallpaper books from home furnishing, paint or hardware stores. Give children sheets of floral print wallpaper. Direct them to cut out flowers, glue on construction paper and add leaves and stems to create Mary's garden.

B. Give each child a paper muffin cup to glue to a sheet of construction paper. Direct children to draw a stem and leaves.

SCIENCE

Bring easy-to-grow flower seeds (marigolds, etc.) to class. Help children plant the seeds in paper cups. Water when dry and keep in a sunny place. The children will enjoy watching "Mary's garden" grow.

ORAL LANGUAGE DEVELOPMENT
What did Mary have? What did she have in it?

FIELD TRIP
Visit a florist, a greenhouse or a nursery to introduce plants and flowers to the children. Purchase seeds and plants for your classroom. Let children help you take care of the plants.

DRAMA
Ask for volunteers to play the roles of Mary, the silver bells (and seeds), the cockle shells (and seeds) and the pretty maids. The volunteers pantomime the rhyme following these directions.

"Mary" plants "seeds" (actors playing seeds must curl up as small as possible). When "Mary" waters the "seeds," they grow slowly until they are standing tall. The "flowers" move in the wind and the "pretty maids" dance in and out between the flowers. (As an extra, play "Waltz of the Flowers" from "The Nutcracker Suite" to enhance this experience.)

MUSIC
Play the following on a piano or guitar, and teach the song to the children.

   G G G E
Mistress Mary

    G G G D
Quite contrary

    C   D   E   F A G
How does your garden grow?

    C   B C   A
With silver bells

   A   A B   G
And cockle shells

    C F G   D   E E D C
And pretty maids all in a row.

ACTIVITY SHEET
Reproduce and use.

MISTRESS MARY

WEE WILLIE WINKIE

Wee Willie Winkie runs through the town,
Upstairs and downstairs in his night-gown,
Rapping at the window, crying through the lock,
"Are the children all in bed, for now it's eight o'clock?"

HISTORY: "Wee Willie Winkie" was a nickname given to William, Prince of Orange. It was not intended to have any political significance.

Activities

ART (SEWING)
Willie's Stocking Cap
Cut soft flannel material into triangles large enough to fit on a child's head. Give 2 to each child. Help the children sew, staple or glue the 2 sides together, leaving the bottom open so the completed cap will fit on a child's head.

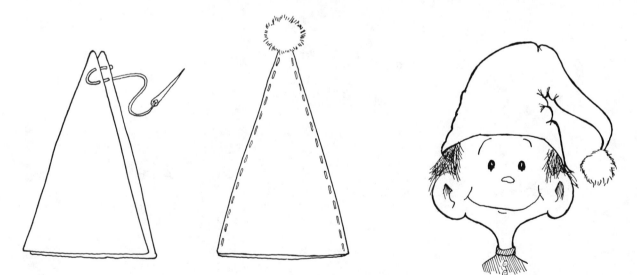

Add a yarn ball or pompom to the end of the cap.

SPECIAL ACTIVITY
Pajama Day
When the weather is warm enough, ask children to wear their pajamas to school (or bring them and change at school). They may also enjoy bringing their teddy bears or other nighttime companions. Have some bedtime stories on hand (*Bedtime for Francis* is a good one). Talk about the different kinds of pajamas and stuffed animals. It's also a good time to discuss bedtime health practices (brushing teeth, washing face, etc.).

ORAL LANGUAGE DEVELOPMENT

Where did Willie run? What did he wear? What did he do? What did he say? What time was it?

CONCEPTS

Through   Upstairs   Downstairs

DRAMA

Take the children to a place where they have access to a set of stairs. Dramatize the rhyme by letting 1 child run upstairs and downstairs while the other children pretend to be sleeping.

MUSIC GAME

Choose 1 child to be "Willie." "Willie" sings, "Are you sleeping, Are you sleeping, little one, little one?" to each child (tune, "Are You Sleeping?"). Each child answers "Yes, Wee Willie, Yes, Wee Willie, It's eight o'clock, eight o'clock." After singing the part, each child puts head down on hands.

ACTIVITY SHEET

Reproduce and use.

46

WEE WILLIE WINKIE

OLD MOTHER HUBBARD

Old Mother Hubbard
Went to the cupboard
To fetch her poor dog a bone.
But when she got there
The cupboard was bare
And so the poor dog had none.

HISTORY: "Old Mother Hubbard" was a stock nursery tale character, but the verses as we know them today were created by Sarah Catherine Martin, circa 1804.

Activities

ART
Give the children pre-cut construction paper cupboards. Let them look through magazines to find and cut out a Mother Hubbard and a dog. Glue the cupboard onto paper; put Mother Hubbard inside and the dog outside.

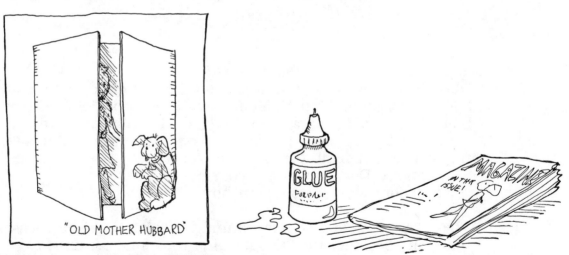

ORAL LANGUAGE DEVELOPMENT
Who went to the cupboard? What did she find there? Who wanted a bone? What did the dog get?

DRAMA
Paint a large cardboard box to resemble a cupboard. Ask for volunteers for the roles of Mother Hubbard and the dog. Encourage "Mother Hubbard" and the "dog" to show expressions of surprise and dismay as the rest of the children recite the rhyme. Ask the children how they think the dog felt. Ask them to show sad faces and hungry faces.

GAME

A. *Stock the Cupboard*

Direct the children to sit in the circle. Ask 1 child to volunteer to be "Mother Hubbard" and to sit in the center of the circle. "Mother Hubbard" says, "Who will help me fill my cupboard?" and points to a child. The child tells what he/she will add to the bare cupboard. As the game continues, each child must tell what all the other children have given and then add his/her contribution.

Example: The first child says, "I will give you cookies." The second child says, "I will give you cookies and apples." The third child says, "I will give you cookies, apples and chocolate cake," etc.

B. *Doggie, Doggie, Where's Your Bone?*

Obtain a rubber bone from a pet store. Ask 1 child to volunteer to be the "doggie." Seat children in a circle with the "doggie" in the center with the bone in front of him/her. The "doggie" closes his/her eyes. A child from the circle quietly comes and steals the bone. When the child is reseated with the bone out of sight, the children call,

"Doggie, Doggie, where's your bone?
Someone stole it from your home!"

The "doggie" gets 3 guesses to find the thief. If he/she guesses correctly, that child becomes the "doggie" and the game continues.

ACTIVITY SHEET

Reproduce and use.

OLD MOTHER HUBBARD

THE OLD WOMAN
WHO LIVED IN A SHOE

There was an old woman who lived in a shoe.
She had so many children she didn't know what to do.
She gave them some broth without any bread.
She whipped them all soundly and put them to bed.

HISTORY: Some experts believe the "old woman" to be Parliament, which "lived in a shoe" (the British Isles) and ruled the "so many children" of its vast empire.

ART

Give the children 2 tagboard shoe patterns to trace on construction paper and cut out. Staple the 2 shoes together, leaving the top open. Punch holes and insert yarn for laces.

Give students patterns of gingerbread-shaped children that will fit inside the shoe. Ask the children to color them and add faces.

Direct students to count the children as they put them into the shoes.

COOKING

Make "Old Woman Broth" for your children by following this recipe.

2 10½ oz. cans condensed beef broth	1 soup can of water
1/4 cup sliced carrots	1/4 cup sliced celery
2 sprigs parsley	1 small bay leaf

1/4 teaspoon thyme leaves

Heat all ingredients to boiling. Reduce heat, cover and simmer for 30 minutes, and then strain. Serve with a slice of bread and butter (or crackers) to make your children feel special.

LIFE SKILLS

Seat the children in a circle and discuss the different kinds of shoes (buckle, tie, sneakers, sandals, etc.). Ask children to point to the sole, tongue, heel, laces, bow, knot, etc. How many shoes make a pair? Which is your left shoe? Your right shoe? How are your parents' shoes different from yours?

ORAL LANGUAGE DEVELOPMENT

Who lived in a shoe? How would you like to live in a shoe? (Ask the children to dictate stories to you about life in a shoe.)

MUSIC

Play the following on a guitar or piano, and teach the tune to the children.

     High
A B   C A A B A
There was an old woman

    High
A   C AA B
Who lived in a shoe;

 A G F B B B# A
She had so many children

 B B B F   B B B
She didn't know what to do;

    High High High   High High High
A B C   D   E B   C D DE B
She gave them some broth without any bread

High
C D E   A A A G A E F G A
She whipped them all soundly and put them to bed.

DRAMA

Ask for volunteers for the roles of the old woman and some of her children. Another group of children form a circle to create the shoe. Use bowls, a ladle and a pot for props. Direct the actors to pantomime the rhyme as the other children recite it.

GAME

Every child takes off one shoe and puts it in a pile with the other shoes. Two children race against each other to see who can first find his/her shoe, put it on and return to the group. (Give extra points if the shoes are tied.)

ACTIVITY SHEET

Reproduce and use.

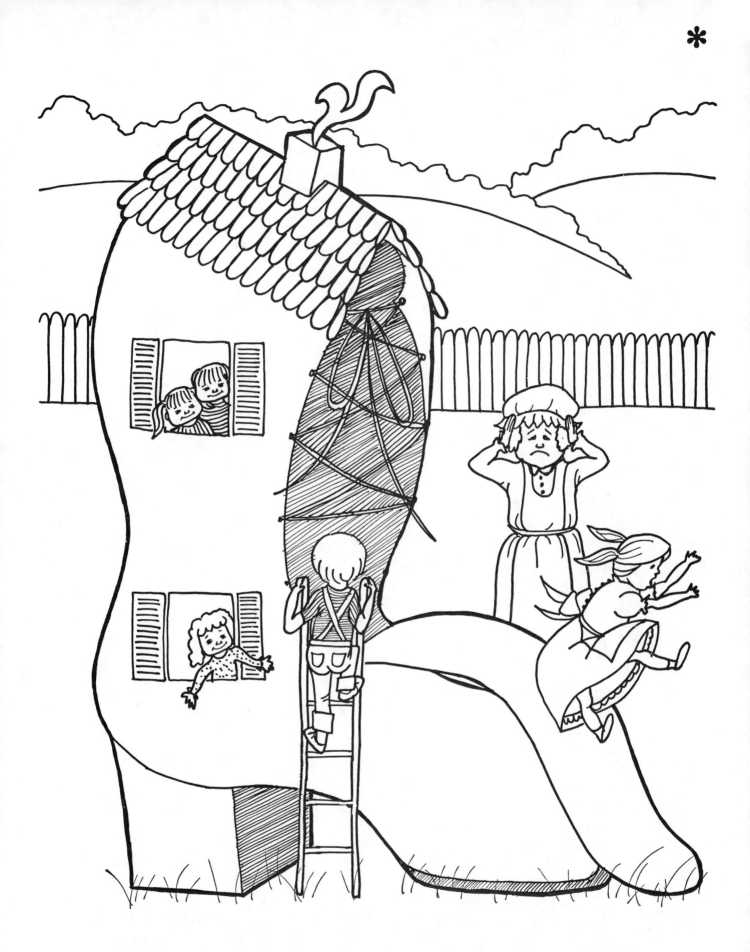

THE OLD WOMAN WHO LIVED IN A SHOE

LITTLE BOY BLUE

Little Boy Blue,
    Come blow your horn,
The sheep's in the meadow,
    The cow's in the corn.

Where is the boy
    Who looks after the sheep?
He's under the haystack
    Fast asleep.

Will you wake him?
    No, not I!
For if I do,
    He's sure to cry.

HISTORY: "Little Boy Blue" has been identified with Thomas, Cardinal Wolsey, son of a wealthy butcher, who as a child, looked after his father's sheep. In more recent times, the poem was well known as a popular lullaby.

Activities

ART

A. Collect large cardboard tubes and let children paint them. When the tubes are dry, cover one end with a piece of tissue paper, and secure with a rubber band.

   Let children blow into one end to "call" the cow and sheep.

B. Illustrate the rhyme on a large sheet of mural paper.

COOKING

To make *Peanut Haystacks*, follow this recipe.

1 tablespoon smooth peanut butter	1 cup roasted peanuts
1 3 oz. can "Chow Mein" noodles	1 6 oz. package butterscotch morsels

Melt peanut butter and butterscotch morsels together in a heavy saucepan over low heat. Add noodles and peanuts to mixture, and mix until well coated. Form little clusters on foil and set in refrigerator to harden. Makes 24 haystacks.

LIFE SKILLS

Boil corn on the cob in salted water until tender. Serve with butter, salt and pepper. While the children are enjoying the corn, discuss the words *husk*, *cornsilk*, *kernels* and *tassels*.

ORAL LANGUAGE DEVELOPMENT

What instrument did the little boy have? Where was the little boy? Where were the sheep? Where was the cow?

CHORAL SPEAKING

Select 2 children to be the 2 narrators. Then, teach the rhyme to the children following this format.

Narrator #1:	Little Boy Blue, Come blow your horn,
Narrator #2:	The sheep's in the meadow; The cow's in the corn.
Narrators #1 and #2:	Where is the boy Who looks after the sheep?
Class:	He's under the haystack, Fast asleep.
Narrator #1:	Will you wake him?
Narrator #2:	No, not I!
Class:	For if I do, He's sure to cry.

MUSIC

Use a piano or guitar to play the following tune. Teach it to the children, and let them sing it with you.

D G E   F   E   D   E F
Little Boy Blue, come blow your horn.

E   D   G A B A G B A G B
The sheep's in the meadow, the cow's in the corn.

High   High
  D   B G   E   E   E   C A F   D
Where is the boy who looks after the sheep?

        High High
  G F F G D C B A G
He's under the haystack fast asleep.

ACTIVITY SHEET

Reproduce and use.

LITTLE BOY BLUE

RUB-A-DUB-DUB

Rub-a-dub-dub,
Three men in a tub,
And who do you think they be?
The butcher, the baker,
*   the candlestick maker ...*
Turn them out, knaves all three!

HISTORY: The rhyme originally read "three maids in a tub," with the butcher, the baker and the candlestick maker being onlookers, probably at a questionable fair sideshow.

Activities

ART
Collect a plastic margarine container for each child. Let children use tempera paints to paint the tubs and cut pictures of 3 people from catalogs or magazines to represent the butcher, baker and candlestick maker. Place in tub.

FIELD TRIP
Visit a grocery story and watch a butcher at work, or visit a bakery.

ORAL LANGUAGE DEVELOPMENT
How many men were in the tub? What were their jobs? What does a butcher do? What does a baker do? What other rhyme do you know that has a candlestick in it?

MUSIC

Sing the rhyme with the children to the tune of "Michael, Row the Boat Ashore."

Rub-a-dub-dub, three men in a tub; allelu-u-ja
Rub-a-dub-dub, three men in a tub; allelu-u-ja
And who do you-u think they be? allelu-u-ja
And who do you-u think they be? allelu-u-ja
The butcher, baker and candlestick maker   allelu-u-ja
The butcher, baker and candlestick maker   allelu-u-ja
Turn them out, knaves all three!   allelu-ja
Turn them out, knaves all three!   allelu-u-ja

RHYME STUDY

Ask children to come up with words that will finish the following.

Rub-a-dub-DOT, three men in a _____.
Rub-a-dub-DOO, three men in a _____.
Rub-a-dub-DIP, three men in a _____.
Rub-a-dub-DEE, three men in a _____.

DRAMA

Use a wooden rocking boat, or paint a large carton to resemble a boat. Let the class sing the above song as 3 children ride in the boat. Be sure all children have a turn in the boat.

ACTIVITY SHEET

Reproduce and use.

RUB-A-DUB-DUB

THREE BLIND MICE

Three blind mice,
Three blind mice,
See how they run,
See how they run!
They all ran after the farmer's wife,
Who cut off their tails with a carving knife.
Did you ever see such a sight in your life
As three blind mice?

HISTORY: Since the 19th century, this has been a favorite round song of English-speaking children, and is probably the best known nursery rhyme extant.

Activities

ART
Ask children to illustrate the rhyme by drawing the 3 mice and the farmer's wife. Give each child 3 pieces of yarn to use for the mice's tails.

MAGNET BOARD STORY
Find a picture of a woman to represent the farmer's wife. Cut mice shapes from construction paper and attach yarn tails. Attach a paper clip to the back of each figure so that they will be attracted to a magnetized board. Let children take turns "working" the board as they repeat the rhyme.

ORAL LANGUAGE DEVELOPMENT
What is the plural of *mouse*? (One mouse, three ___?___) Who cut off their tails?
What did the mice do? What did the farmer's wife use to cut off the mice's tails?

DRAMA
Ask for volunteers to play the roles of the 3 mice and the farmer's wife. Use
blindfolds, a cardboard knife and yarn tails for props.

GAME
The Blind Mouse

Children stand in a circle surrounding one child who has been blindfolded (the
"blind mouse"). Children come close to the "mouse" to tease him/her, seeing
how close they can come without being caught. When a child is caught by the
"mouse," he or she becomes the "mouse" and is blindfolded.

MUSIC
Play this accompaniment on the piano or guitar as the children sing along.

   F   E   DD F   E   DD
Three blind mice, three blind mice,

 A G G FF A G G FF
See how they run, see how they run!

    High High   High
A   D D C# B C# D A A
They all ran after the farmer's wife,

  A   DD   D C# B C# D A   A
Who cut off their tails with a carving knife.

  A   D D D C# B C# D A A   A
Did you ever see such a sight in your life

  G   F   E   D
As three blind mice!

ACTIVITY SHEET
Reproduce and use.

THREE BLIND MICE

MARY HAD A LITTLE LAMB

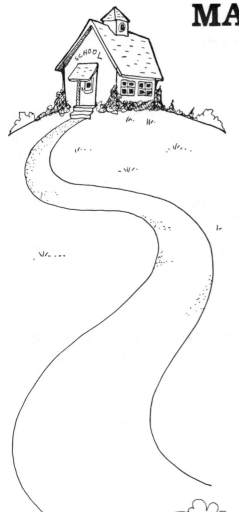

Mary had a little lamb,
*   Its fleece was white as snow;*
And everywhere that Mary went,
*   The lamb was sure to go.*

It followed her to school one day:
*   That was against the rule.*
It made the children laugh and play
*   To see a lamb at school!*

Activities

ART
Help each child trace a lamb pattern onto white construction paper and cut it out.
Provide cotton balls for children to glue onto their lambs for fleece.

ORAL LANGUAGE DEVELOPMENT
What did Mary have? What color was the lamb? Where did the lamb follow Mary?
What did the children do?

RHYME STUDY
Encourage the children to change the verse to give Mary different animals.

    Example: Mary had a little dog,
                 It's fur was black as night;
             And everyone that Mary saw,
                 The dog was sure to bite!

MUSIC

Play this accompaniment on the piano as the children sing the song.

A G F G A A A   G G G   A C C
Mary had a little lamb, little lamb, little lamb.

A G F G A A A A   G   G   A G   F
Mary had a little lamb, its fleece was white as snow.

A   A G   F   G A A   A G G G   A C C
And everywhere that Mary went, Mary went, Mary went,

A G   F   G A A A   A G   G A G F
Everywhere that Mary went, the lamb was sure to go.

DRAMA

Ask for volunteers for the roles of Mary and the lamb. (The rest of the class will be the "children.") Ask the volunteers to pantomime the verse while the children recite it. Emphasize action and facial expressions.

ACTIVITY SHEET

Reproduce and use.

MARY HAD A LITTLE LAMB

LITTLE BO-PEEP

Little Bo-Peep has lost her sheep
And doesn't know where to find them.
Leave them alone and they'll come home
Wagging their tails behind them.

HISTORY: The term "Bo-Peep" could at one time have referred to a nursery activity similar to today's well-known "Peek-A-Boo."

ART

Provide tagboard sheep patterns for children to trace on construction paper. Give separate patterns for large sheep tails.

Instruct the children to cut out their sheep and tails. Then, attach tails to sheep with brads so that the sheep will be able to wag "their tails behind them."

COOKING

Give the children a healthy taste treat with *Bo-Peep's Honey Drink*.

Stir 1½ teaspoons of honey into 1 tall glass of cold milk. Add a touch of cinnamon or nutmeg for a really delicious drink.

ORAL LANGUAGE DEVELOPMENT

What did Bo-Peep lose? Who will come home? What will be wagging behind them? Tell about something you've lost. How did you feel?

CONCEPT

Behind

DRAMA

Ask for volunteers to play the roles of Bo-Peep and her sheep. Encourage Bo-Peep to express sadness as she looks for and calls (in pantomime) her sheep. After Bo-Peep has "looked" for her sheep, they should reappear. Encourage the sheep to show that they are glad to see Bo-Peep.

RHYME STUDY

Read these lines aloud to the children. Encourage them to give the missing rhyming word, and to think of other words (and rhymes for them) to take the place of "Peep."

Little Bo-Pare has lost her ____?____.
Little Bo-Pogg has lost her ____?____.
Little Bo-Pitty has lost her ____?____.
Little Bo-Pird has lost her ____?____.

MUSIC

Play the following accompaniment as the children sing.

High
A D F C B A E F
Little Bo-Peep has lost her sheep

E D D D E F A F
And doesn't know where to find them.

B B B A A G F E
Leave them alone and they'll come home

High High
D C# B A F D E D
Wagging their tails behind them.

ACTIVITY SHEET

Reproduce and use.

74

LITTLE BO-PEEP

OLD KING COLE

Old King Cole
Was a merry old soul,
And a merry old soul was he.
He called for his pipe,
And he called for his bowl,
And he called for his fiddlers three!

HISTORY: This verse may refer to King Cole, an English ruler of the third century, who was known to like fiddle music.

Activities

ART

Give each child a piece of tin foil (or foil wallpaper) from which to create a king's crown. Draw lines on the foil to show children where to cut.

Fit each child and staple ends together.

SCIENCE

Serve the following recipe for *Old King Cole's Delight* to the children.

¼ cantaloupe per child   ice cream to fill   maraschino cherries

Fill each cantaloupe with a scoop of ice cream and top with cherries.

Discuss cantaloupe seeds and how cantaloupes grow. Show pictures to the children of cantaloupes in various growth stages. Experiment by placing some cantaloupe seeds on a wet sponge and others in a paper cup filled with soil. Ask children to watch the seeds to see which will spout first.

ORAL LANGUAGE DEVELOPMENT

Who was a merry old soul? What did the king call for? Who entertained King Cole? What other rhyme do you know that has a fiddle in it?

MOVEMENT

Teach the children the following actions.

Old King Cole was a merry old soul	(Lift elbows up and down)
And a merry old soul was he.	(Nod head vigorously)
He called for his pipe,	(Clap 2 times, then march 12 counts)
And he called for his bowl,	(Clap 2 times, then march 12 counts)
And he called for his fiddlers three!	(Clap 2 times, then bow an arm like a violin and play it with the other)

MUSIC

Play the following on a guitar or piano as children sing along.

Low
```
  B    E    E    F    E F G G    G    F
```
Now old King Cole was a merry old soul

```
  G A B B      E F      D# E
```
And a merry old soul was he.

Low
```
B    B    E    E    F    G    A    B    E    G    F
```
He called for his pipe and he called for his bowl

```
                          Low
G    A B    E    E    F    B    E
```
And he called for his fiddlers three.

DRAMA

Ask for volunteers to play the roles of King Cole, the fiddlers and ladies- (or gentlemen-) in-waiting to bring the pipe and the bowl. Encourage "King Cole" to look "merry."

ACTIVITY SHEET

Reproduce and use.

OLD KING COLE

PUSSY CAT, PUSSY CAT

Pussy cat, pussy cat, where have you been?
I've been to London to look at the Queen.
Pussy cat, pussy cat, what did you there?
I frightened a little mouse under her chair!

HISTORY: Some scholars think that the "Queen" may be Elizabeth I, and that the rhyme refers to an event which actually happened while she was on the throne.

Activities

ART
Let the children find and cut out pictures of cats from greeting cards and magazines. Children paste their cats on pieces of construction paper and then draw the queen, the mouse and the chair. (Teacher help may be needed for this.)

ORAL LANGUAGE DEVELOPMENT
Where had the pussy cat been? What did she frighten? Can you name 3 other words that mean the same thing as *frighten*?

CONCEPT
Under

MUSIC
Teach the children to sing the verse to the following tune.

			High			High		High	High	High	High
C	A	F	C	A	F	C		C	C	C

Pussy cat, pussy cat, where have you been?

G E C G E C G G G
I've been to London to look at the queen

F G A G A Bᵇ F Bᵇ C D
Pussy cat, pussy cat, what did you there?

D D C Bᵇ Bᵇ A G F E D C F
I frightened a little mouse under her chair.

DRAMA

Ask for volunteers to play the roles of the queen, the pussy cat, the mouse and the narrator. Provide a crown and a chair for props. (Encourage the cat to meow and the mouse to squeak during the "chase scene.")

GAMES

A. *Nice Kitty*

One child is chosen to be the "kitty." The rest of the children sit in a circle. As the "kitty" goes to each child in the circle, he/she pets the "kitty" and says, "Nice kitty," but the "kitty" makes no reply. Finally, the "kitty" meows in response to one child. That child must run around the outside of the circle as the "kitty" chases him/her. If that child returns to his/her original place before the "kitty" can catch him/her, that child becomes the new "kitty."

B. *Cat and Mouse*

One child volunteers to be the "cat." The rest of the children are "mice." Designate a post or tree as the "cat's" home and another spot as the mouse hole. The "cat" stays home and the "mice" come to bother him. The cat cannot chase a "mouse" until one touches its home. Then, the "cat" chases that "mouse." If the "cat" catches that "mouse" before it returns to the mouse hole, that "mouse" becomes another "cat" and helps the first "cat" catch other "mice."

ACTIVITY SHEET

Reproduce and use.

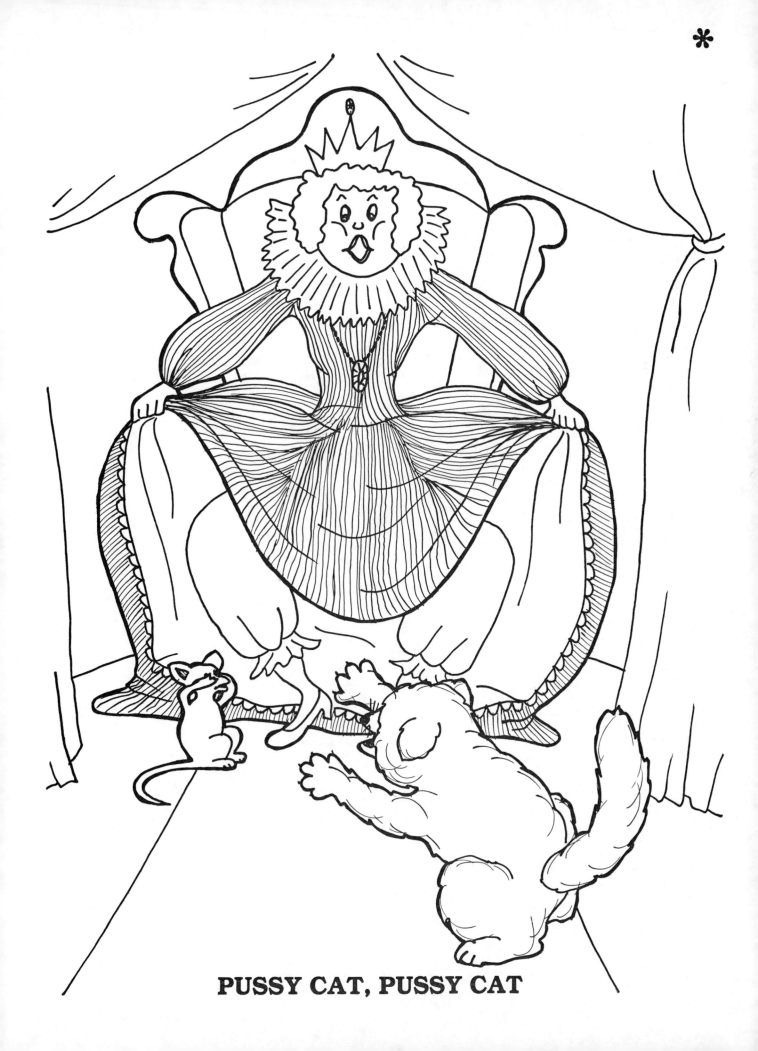

PUSSY CAT, PUSSY CAT

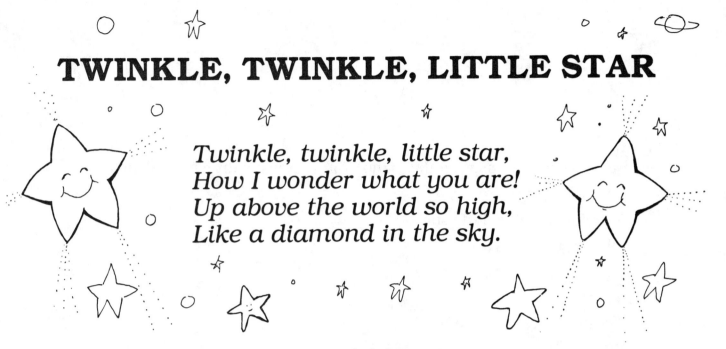

TWINKLE, TWINKLE, LITTLE STAR

Twinkle, twinkle, little star,
How I wonder what you are!
Up above the world so high,
Like a diamond in the sky.

Activities

ART
Give each child a piece of blue construction paper (to represent the night sky) and ask him/her to draw a picture of himself/herself on it. Then, direct the children to add stars to their drawings.

BULLETIN BOARD
Ask children to bring in pictures of themselves. Draw stars on construction paper or tin foil and let the children cut them out. Mount each photograph on a star and staple stars to a bulletin board.

ORAL LANGUAGE DEVELOPMENT
What does the star do? Where is the star? Who wonders? What is the star like? Why? Can you think of another word that means the same thing as *twinkle*?

CONCEPTS
High/Low   Up   Above

FOLLOWING DIRECTIONS
Let each child cut out a paper star. Then, ask the children to listen carefully and follow your directions to place the stars over their heads, above their heads, between their knees, to one side, to the other side, under their chairs, high, low and in the middle.

RHYME STUDY
Ask children to think of words that rhyme with *twinkle*. (crinkle, wrinkle, tinkle) What do the words mean? What crinkles? What wrinkles? What tinkles?

MUSIC

Play this accompaniment on the piano or guitar as children sing along.

F F   C   C   D D C
Twinkle, twinkle, little star

B^b B^b A A   G   G   F
How I wonder what you are.

C C B^b B^b A   A G
Up above the world so high

C C B^b B^b A A G
Like a diamond in the sky

F F   C   C D D C
Twinkle, twinkle, little star

B^b B^b A A   G   G   F
How I wonder what you are

Other star songs you might teach the children are:
"Catch a Falling Star"
"When You Wish Upon a Star"

GAMES

Moon and Twinkling Stars

Ask a child to be the "moon" and stand in a shady spot. All the other children are "twinkling stars." "Stars" come into the shaded area and see how close they can get to the "moon" without being caught. The "moon" tries to catch one of the "stars" before it can return to the safety of sunlight. If the "star" is caught, it becomes the "moon."

ACTIVITY SHEET

Reproduce and use.

TWINKLE, TWINKLE, LITTLE STAR

HICKORY DICKORY DOCK

Hickory, dickory, dock.
The mouse ran up the clock,
The clock struck one,
The mouse ran down!
Hickory, dickory, dock.

HISTORY: It is possible that the first line is an attempt to render the ticking sounds of a large clock into words. Children are attracted to the rhyme by its clock-like rhythm and the nonsense situation it presents.

Activities

ART

Make a ditto master of a clock face and a mouse. Reproduce one for each child and let children cut out. Paste each clock face on a paper plate.

Punch a hole near the "12." Help each child thread a piece of yarn through the hole and attach one end to the mouse so that the mouse can run up and down the clock when the child pulls the thread.

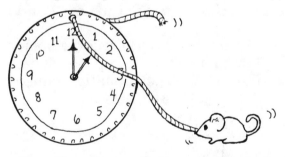

RHYME STUDY

Encourage the children to come up with other rhyming pairs to substitute in the verse.

Examples: Hickory, Dickory, Doo,
A mouse ran up my _____.

Hickory, Dickory, Dan,
A mouse ran up my _____.

Hickory, Dickory, Dap,
A mouse ran up my _____.

Hickory, Dickory, Dup,
A mouse ran up my _____.

Hickory, Dickory, Dip,
A mouse ran up my _____.

ORAL LANGUAGE DEVELOPMENT

Who ran up the clock? Who ran down the clock? Where did the mouse run? What time was it when the mouse ran down?

MOVEMENT

Teach the children these movements to accompany the rhyme.

Hickory, Dickory, Dock   (Bend low and swing arms)
The mouse ran up the clock   (Stretch up with arms high)
The clock struck one;   (Clap 1 time)
The mouse ran down.   (Bend down)
Hickory, Dickory, Dock.   (Swing arms)

MUSIC

Sing the rhyme to the tune of "London Bridge Is Falling Down."

Hickory, Dickory, Dickory, Dock
The mouse ran up, up the clock.
The clock struck one; the mouse ran down.
Hickory, Dickory, Do-ock.

GAME

Provide a working alarm clock that ticks at normal volume. Set the alarm to go off at a pre-determined time and hide it. Tell the children that they are mice looking for the clock. If a child finds the clock before the alarm goes off, reward him/her with cheese kisses. If the alarm goes off first, the children get no rewards.

ACTIVITY SHEET

Reproduce and use.

HICKORY DICKORY DOCK

RHYME REVIEW

Who sat on a wall?
Who sat on a tuffet?
Who sat in a corner?
Who lived in a pumpkin shell?
Who put her there?
Who lived in a shoe?
Who frightened Miss Muffet?
Who frightened a mouse under the queen's chair?
Who fell down the hill?
Who fell off the wall?
Who had 3 bags full?
What animals belonged to Little Bo-Peep?
What animal belonged to Mother Hubbard?
How many blind mice were there?
How many fiddlers did Old King Cole have?
How many people were in a tub?
Which rhymes have musical instruments?
What did Miss Muffet eat?
What did the children who lived in a shoe eat?
What did Little Jack Horner eat?
What did Peter, Peter eat?
Who had a garden?
Who had a candlestick?
What time was it in "Wee Willie Winkie"?
What time was it when the mouse ran down the clock in "Hickory, Dickory, Dock"?
Which rhymes have mice in them?
Which rhymes have cows in them?
Which rhymes have sheep or lambs in them?
What did the cow jump over?
What did Jack jump over?
What is "like a diamond in the sky"?

RHYME GAMES

Children sit in a circle with the teacher in the center. The teacher says a simple
word, such as *hill*, and asks a child to say a word that rhymes with it. The teacher
continues asking for rhyming words from the children until no one can think of
another rhyming word. The teacher then chooses another word and begins again.

Say a rhyme to a child, leaving the last line for the child to say alone from
memory.

Direct the children to clap each rhyme as they repeat it.

"GOOSE EGGS"

Plan a "healthy" menu to suit each nursery rhyme character. (Little Boy Blue might like a picnic lunch of cheese, fruit and bread. Old King Cole would probably enjoy a palace feast with foods from each of the 4 basic food groups.)

Think of something that would have been of great help to each nursery rhyme character in his or her particular situation. (Little Miss Muffett could have killed the spider if she had had a can of insect spray!)

Play "Nursery Rhyme Charades." Assign as many children as needed to each rhyme, and let them pantomime it for the group. The rest of the children try to guess which rhyme each group is portraying.

Let children make nursery rhyme booklets using their completed activity pages. Provide folded construction paper covers for them to decorate, and staple the pages inside. Children will enjoy taking the booklets home to share with their families.

Stage a costume parade. Have each child dress as one of the nursery rhyme characters. Children may sing the various nursery rhyme songs they have learned as they march. Invite another class or parents to come and enjoy the show.

What happened to each character after the events described in his or her rhyme? (What did Jack do about his broken crown? Where did the mouse go after it ran down the clock?)

Put on a TV interview show. Select a moderator (or the teacher could play this part). Let each child choose a character to impersonate. The moderator interviews each character to get his/her viewpoint on the events that took place in his/her rhyme.

Play "Wrong Rhyme." Ask children to think about what would happen if a character found himself or herself in the wrong setting. (What if Old King Cole found himself tumbling down the hill with Jack and Jill? What if Mistress Mary found herself in Old Mother Hubbard's cupboard?)

BIBLIOGRAPHY

Books About Nursery Rhymes And Their Histories

The Annotated Mother Goose by William S. and Ceil Baring-Gould. (Bramhall House)

Early Children's Books and Their Illustrations by Gerald Gottlieb. (David R. Godine)

The Oxford Nursery Rhyme Book by Iona and Peter Opie. (Oxford University Press)

Readings about Children's Literature edited by Evelyn R. Robinson. (David McKay)

Sharing Literature with Children by Francelia Butler. (Longman)

Children's Books

And So My Garden Grows illustrated by Peter Spier. (Doubleday)

Appley Dapply's Nursery Rhymes illustrated by Beatrix Potter. (Frederick Warne)

Brian Wildsmith's Mother Goose illustrated by Brian Wildsmith. (Watts)

Book of Mother Goose and Nursery Rhymes illustrated by Marguerite De Angeli. (Doubleday)

Frank Baber's Mother Goose selected by R. Spriggs. (Crown)

In a Pumpkin Shell illustrated by Joan Walsh Anglund. (Harcourt)

Lavender Blue compiled by Kathleen Lines; illustrated by Harold Jones. (Watts)

Mother Goose illustrated by Frederick Richardson. (Hubbard)

Mother Goose illustrated by Tasha Tudor. (Walck)

Mother Goose and Nursery Rhymes illustrated by Philip Reed. (Atheneum)

The Mother Goose Book illustrated by Alice and Martin Provensen. (Random House)

Mother Goose: The Old Nursery Rhymes illustrated by Arthur Rackham. (Century)

Ring O' Roses illustrated by Leslie Brook. (Warne)

Sing Mother Goose illustrated by Marjorie Torrey. (Dutton)

The Tall Book of Mother Goose illustrated by Feodor Rojankovsky. (Harper)

The White Land illustrated by Raymond Briggs. (Coward)

LETTING LOOSE ON
MOTHER GOOSE